Dancing with the Moon

Dancing with the Moon

Poems of the Heart

by

Steven Dale Davison

Cover photograph by Aron Visuals, instagram.com/aronvisuals
Author photograph by Christine M. Lewandoski

ISBN: 978-1-63980-355-2

Kelsay Books
502 South 1040 East, A-119
American Fork, Utah 84003
Kelsaybooks.com

for Christine, my wife,
my evermuse

Acknowledgments

The following poems have been published previously, although in different versions in some cases:

Comstock Review: "Who Loves You Not"
Crosswinds: "Moving Out"
Gravitas: "Animal Words," "The Kiss"
Inscape: "The Perseids"
Maximum Tilt: "He's Tall," "Thank You"
River and South: "Trail Maker"
Sixfold: "A Sleepless Sense of Found," "O My Heart," "Sowise,"
  "Wordsmouth Harbor Founder," "You Are Leaving"

Dancing with the Moon is a re-conception and expansion of a chapbook of love poems published in May 2022 by Moonstone Press titled *O My Heart.* Twenty-five of the poems in *Dancing with the Moon* also appeared in *O My Heart.*

The following poems were also published as brief love poem interludes in my collection of "nature" poems *Dancing Mockingbird,* published in February 2022 by Kelsay Books—

Kelsay Books: "Animal Words," "A Sleepless Sense of Found,"
  "Do Moths Not Know?," "Love's Lost Demesne," "Mojo
  Clover," "The Perseids," "Trail Maker," "You Are Leaving,"
  "Deep-Water Eyes" (under the title "You Mountains and Deep
  Water")

Phases of Moontide

What Are We?

Yours the New Smile

You Move Me

The World Knows Its Meaning

You Rhyme Every Sound

Overture

Dancing with the Moon

For three score years and more
I've been dancing with the moon,
answering her tide-pull on my heart
with my homing hopes and pen.
With these words upon the page
I have tracked its arcs of wonderment.
I have thrilled to the lift of that
first wave of attraction.
I have felt its promise slip away
or buoy me with new connection.
And then, oh then, the satisfaction,
the years of recording the bounty swells
beneath her blessèd call—
only to know again the lash
of storm and break-up, after all.
Thrown once more into the thrashing roil,
I seize some flotsam in desperation
and drift, clinging to memories and regret.
I pray for rescue. And yet, I write.

Once the sea has calmed after wreckage
and the boiling clouds have cleared,
and I have spied some solid land,
a new captivation beckons from the strand.
My pen reckons once again with hope
and the cycle begins anew. New promises
are filled or unfulfilled, new relationships
enjoyed and then dissolved, until
the one.

Here the journey finds its homeland.
Here a haven holds my thankful habitation.
With new stanzas I exult in the sacrament
ultimate. Storms still batter, yes. But even

in the howling night I still can see the beacon.
I still know the reason why I married,
and in the light of the goddess moon, I dance.
We dance.

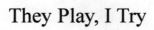

They Play, I Try

Mirrors of Duet: They Play

she holds   off
    head tilt eyeshade and curiosity
        dis   stance   sing

he bolds on
    voice lilt smile and hopeful mimery
        into   it   ing

they play   they may
    take it to the hilt if she feels
        does   wonders   he

Mirrors of Duet: He's Tall

He's tall,
        dark,
                well,
he's just barely handsome,
    hair thick and trying to be—
    full frame but not quite—.
He moves over
              right next
                  then . . .
With a smile he mimes lighting
the Fantasy Lucky she raises to her lips.
She takes a long deep and lifts her chin.
The jazz moves her elbow, and
she nudges into his must
    be made of light and honey,
    so bright his eyes . . .
So,
    hi's,
        and, yes, she thinks she
        could just float and sink and—
How far?
    Just—
How long?
    Could—
Would he be
    as gentle as sighs and so strong,
    as sure as time and so good,
    as suave and slow and—

She takes another drag.

Mirrors of Duet: The Dream Tears Free

She's seated alone for two drinks now;
he's seated alone for who knows how many.
He decides it all rides on being bold.
A mindform is born of one light touch
of elbows and eyes caught
in the mirror behind the bar.
He shifts and smiles,
the ice breaks,
the smile takes,
the heart flies
and aches . . .

So strong are the forlorn years,
the dream tears free.
    How far?
      How long?
        Whose car . . .

He orders another margarita.

Mirrors of Duet: Hipsmoove

The Prince of Denmark's dead.
The actors have got their notes,
and I'm sat here with Margarita.
The bass poons cool in the jazz
with piano.
          "Martini bianco,"
she smooths in her foreign voice;
the bartender's never heard.
"But they have them in the Netherlands."

Our eyes meet in the mirror
behind the bar, a wary depth
in how she raises her regard chin,
a counterpoint to how she turns
her body towards me,
hipsmoove as bass lines . . .
I might be falling in.

Mirrors of Duet—Coda: Only These If-Onlys

Were you just two weeks here from Amsterdam?
Around the rim of a maelstrom I spin.
I dream of falling in, of following you—
but such dares make for dizzy disaster.
Looking back that long halfmoon's passage,
its tide'surge waves of hands and lips
slip down shores of daze desire and riptide out.
The swell heaves open the heart we shared,
bares it to the storm. Now the moon's ink
tears these pages with its savage pen,
leaving only these if-onlys.

When You Return

To what enflighted species are we tied, then,
to circle thus at such close distances,
and yet to wait?

When you return from all the 'motions that you've tried,
will we meet again in the middle air
and finally alight?

Who?

Who am I?
Just a friend who walks the Benny dog,
a free ticket to the plays,
and someone to pay for dinner?

Who are you?
Now you've kissed me more than twice,
do you too fly some dream
beyond a short and sweet "Good night"?

Who are we?
Could we ride our limbs to pleasure sation,
tie our lives to hope, and find
the full fill and meant for—?

She's a Sword Dancer

She's a Sword Dancer.
Join her. But beware!
She wields bright cold flame
with her arms in arcs
in acts of self-attentive love.
Her feet sweep, too,
until you totter like a top
and spill into the
       quick cut.

You can't watch your step with her.
You must come into the tango
with your feet skin-shod,
your eyes unhypnotized
by the blade. Then dance
so hard your soles rise up
from the ground-bound floor—
       but no more!
           Or . . .
               But—

A Sleepless Sense of Found

The Kiss

mist
motionless
presses close
upon the soft
open face
of the lake
in the dark
in the chill
in the deep
night quiet
the white still nimbus
clings to lambency
longs against gravity
for the caress to last
until the moon spills
her revelation light

just so
this memory
haunts my lips
the moist imprint
the sensate moment
our mouths barely parted
hovering there—near—in
finitessimal quivers
vivid though hours
have passed—I'm lost
in the mnemesis
of unvoiced promises
and luctance
o the kiss
a liquid fire
all elation night

Memory Flo

I hold the memories
on the surfaces of my fingers,
in the angles my knuckles articulate
as the 'membered strokes pause
here, there, and where . . .

All next day the moments play
the slender curves of firm
beneath the smooth,
then, now, and when

my thoughts linger on
your smile and your laughter,
on the before, the while, and the after,

until I'm quivering once again, and
you are on my mind.

Your Light Is in My Eyes

We amble slowly and yousually talk
or pause among the rocks and
blueming irises. It is early even now.
The slanting sun May light the park
while the shadows lip the long, slow dark
up from the shallows in the river,
from the undersides of bats' wings
aflit about the hill. The mockingbird sing.
I would sit here till I steep and sink
into the silvering sable of your hair,
until my hope is able deep
inside the words you share.
Then, rapt, I laugh and rise with you
to walk and talk some more,
while up the nightfall soars the moon
to shine your light into my eyes.

We Life Time in Manhattan

Uptown, the deep rock bones lie far beneath the ghostgrass
where the wind softly waves through the now-buried blades.

Other lives once moved across those vanished island meadows:
the shadow of a lanky ploughman falls upon the curling furrow,
    while the spinner stops to muse at her wheel.

Midtown, the bedrock base for deco spires remembers
the cool thin cover of earth above and tree roots turning on its face.

Later, new lives learn the names of now-cobbled streets
and cross them to hail the clattering coach,
    dodging the drying patties with practiced feet.

Downtown, the bare rock breaches the surface in places,
lifts its faces to the salty air and throws pebbles on the beaches.

Years and years those lives cross to join us as we walk,
me matching your long strides. We talk about
    life and time and the city's capacity for memory.

Deep down, New York never forgets the fundaments
that give the sky its lines, or its teeming convergence of lifetimes.

We take the table by the window. The waiter opens up our wine.
The conversation burrows deep. The food comes.
    We listen for the reasons why our lives intertwine.

We fanta-see you moving through the trees, standing by a wall
    of low-piled stone to call the ploughman home,
        your red hair blowing in the ancient evening breeze
            of Manhattan.

The Perseids

On the mountain pond the stars
step out onto water obsidian
smooth, a dark as deep
as star beams are lean.

The dome above revolves,
the last indigo fading
into background black
for the wheeling constellations.

As lightquiet counterpoint
to bullfrog songs, the moon
rises. A loon cries. The restless
winds lay down their sighs.

Through the night we doze,
awaken, snug deeper in our bag,
watch the soundless Perseids streak
in extra terra visitation.

Sparks onto Tinder

Besides the overall—
    of a small woman
    full of quick, bright energy
    from deep currents drawn;
    form trim, not taut, loose to move—
with a sense of sparks falling
onto willing tinder, I noticed hair
    from this side of tawn to silver-white
    through wheat and honey,
    falling half-wild in curls
    attuned to quick head-snaps and laughter;
then the limbs:
    full, firm forearms,
    long frame shank of humerus
    holding muscles toned articulate
    to one of the sexiest shapes I've ever seen.

Not yet brazen enough to stare and memorize
the shapes and shades inside your eyes,
I do recall from stolen glances
    point-burst rays of sorrel fanning from a well,
    mixed with pine and wine-reds,
    spraying through a field of grey
    toward a thin dark band unusual.

    And now,
the soft press of hand on skin,
    here and here burned in
    by the slow embrace,
the smell of smoke,
    the sudden heat,
      the tiny flame
        one beat old and holding.

You Wine of Winter's Yearning

As the blacks and whites and many greys
give bright to the bobbing flights of cardinals
and the crimson beads on holly trees,
all your several scholar's chairs, your natty suits
and drawn-back silver hair give ground
to your trim and spinning maenad figure
dancing party nights away; or your eyes
are found to hold the smolder seeds of fire.
Against the sky-wide blues, the bare tree limbs
weave filigrees in overlays of lines
and days grow longer. I wonder
at this closer twining, sing you
wine of winter's yearning, and lean my heart
into our season's hopeful gyre.

A Sleepless Sense of Found

Fog gathers as the evening turns to night.
It dissolves the meadow that surrounds us
    'til the oak looms close above us,
    a bower private, quiet, cozy.
As the stars step back behind the mist,
    the curled brown wetted leaves
    stitter down through the branches of the tree.
We lie close together in our bags, talking.
We steep there, we sink deeper into the share
    as points of correspondence pile up
    in layers from our stories.
My hungry tongue and lips turn demure,
    my wonder rises with the hidden moon
    until a sleepless sense of found enfolds me.

Who Loves You Not

I Love the Way You Move

I love
  the way you move through life,
    like some sometimes
    wildly swinging palette
    flinging its colors out
    in gay trajectory
    with no target;
  the way your walking limbs
    splash the invisible blue
    with the hues of your clothes;
  or just your nose,
    the long proud companion
    of your mischievous eyes;
  the daily surprise
    of your tawny muss;
  the secret fuss
    behind your gifts;
  the way we fit
    when our body shifts.

Body Vows

o my tongue your lips savor
yes my hands your vast lavish
your neck my nuzzle scents
your irises fill my eyes
all these avid sounds
we answer with our body vows
then and now
              and every

Deep-Water Eyes

I lie here, your heat soaking into me.
Alive to my body as the sky over water
certain moments lay, as smooth as mist settling,
as quiet as light. Then, in sleep as hallowed
as the halls of Avalon are my dreams of you.
After the sinking moon drinks of lake
and the sun rises, I awake to the blue
and deep-water eyes of you.

Sowise

In cooldim of greygreen a beenman
    is grinseen, a newway to followfoot.
The woodsing a feeltune. The moonroots
    of shoots an liveseed are wingloose
and bringhymn to yourside in loomlight
    in mineseye. Tremblesure, our wesong
is heartlong, rises in treebreezes and leaves,
    is strong and sowise, so . . .

Thank You

So, you,
in this little flurry of blurry life, are there.
In the storm's surcease you offer me some beer,
and for an evening before the rush begins again
you quip with me in your easy, self-reliant way,
giving me your more than friendship,
and I remember to say
      thank you.

Animal Words

Thick fog denses a pirouette in freeze-time.
    Sound and distance founder, lost in mist and soft, dark air.
The far line of the white ice is lost in the murk-mime,
    the sand sill looms silver on the frozen lip of the lake, there.
I hear your voice from farther up the carriage line,
    too soft to catch the words. A horse coughs in answer.
When I find you, the mare swings her face toward mine
    and you turn, your hand upon her flank, ever the dancer.
I brace to your breaths upon my cheeks. You speak
    animal words that make me laugh and give me thrills.
I am rendered roan and randy, stallion sleek,
    and shivering in my withers, atremble at the thills.
You lean in close to scent my must and smile,
then stamp your foot and whinny, all tease and beguile.

Who Loves You Not

I sing a song for your clear grey eyes and wise ways,
for your touch and little gifts that lift the spirit,
for ears that really listen, kissing even my absurdities;
for words of ease to a father bothered by the cares
that wear so at your own motherhood; and other good traits
that time cultivates in such fine soil: toil with mirth,
its real worth valued, blending humor with labor,
and yet a saber ready for the fray against the bray of asses.
Quickly passes the time when valentines are due,
and you do not fit into this little piece of poem—
I'm not going to finish this thinnish ode
to all your graces. Some praises, though late,
perforce must wait till eyes and lips can meet,
then greet you strong with the truth immediate:
who loves you not is proved an idiot.

Our Time Has a Tick

Do Moths Not Know?

Do moths not know?

I've heard flames
look like the moon to them,
calling to their benighted brains
with silent siren light—
at a distance the moon's face shines
with a lover's pale promises;
but the tongues of fire, they deliver
a nemesis in immanence,
an ecstasis plunge into
a seductive, razing bright.

I put all the warning words behind me.
I rode my willing wings of hope
'til I was face to face with blaze,
your waxing smile fatale. Yes, I
sped my pace and heart-long flew
into your beck and goad beguile—
and then my wings exploded.

Up their sizzling cinders drift now
in the wronglift of a torch song plume,
a shroud of cloud across the moon.

Our Time Has a Tick

Our time has a tick and misses much.
Momentary holes appear
and kisses drain away.
Fingers catch in sudden cracks
that trick the reaching touch.
A smile bounces off the mirror flesh,
evades the hungry eyes.
The taste of desire turns sour.
Sighs burn to wisps of smoke
and drift into the silence.
The minute hand measures hours,
each little click a falling-to of latch,
a closing of closeness,
a tock of blissless match.

The Grievance Rack

You keep a many-peggèd grievance rack
in the parlor of your heart, that part
of our life we spend so much time in.
It feels out of place there.
Why not in the closet, where
it would not take up any space
that greener thoughts might live in.
But no—red and blue and black,
rage and resentment, even hate—
you need to keep these garments
in your view, close to mind,
ready to wear, easy to find.

Your Rage

Your rage,
one justice crimson raze,
abandons all the other elements
to plunge into the only blaze
your body vows to suffer.

I, Manrat

The terrier terror is on my tail;
I've made some mistake.
I race across open ground,
knowing there is no bolt hole.
She shouts out my name
and surges closer.
I turn to face my fate. She lunges.
Her teeth sink in. She shakes me
till she breaks my error's back.
I do not squeal; I will not heal.
She trots into her temple's inner court
lolling my limp and bleeding form.
She lays me on the altar
of her goddess's judging scorn.

Mojo Clover

I am lid-thick since receiving
your four-leaf clover, as though—
and so I still may be in love with you.
I see the dangers and the fate,
the petals dropping onto ash.
Yet now I drive the long distances.
I will step into the room with my jacket open,
set my suitcase slowly on the floor.
Our seeking eyes will reach—.
I will rush to lift you at the waist,
because I am strong
and you are made of scent,
and a hard kiss will not wait.
We will cut it short for the others,
who are wondering.
But a second kiss will ravage drag us
to another room and throw us on the couch
and plunge us tongue deep into
our cast-off-naked press
of seeming ancient hunger now.
The moment's blazing fails to slake
the questions crawling back and asking,
now what? But a third kiss shall;
arms and hands your ribs engulf,
a little chill now through your dress
upon your arching back,
your golden hair my face all over,
full of nostril flare and sigh,
and not all because of that four-leaf clover—
a purpose void of why.

You Are Leaving

Two Heart Swing

Two hearts swing
                              and sync,
                                    find
a moment,
own
                         the knowing,
                                mind
the timing,
share
                           the wings.
                               Then
two time
flings
                       them off course,
                               can't,
fly too—
close—
                         their wings tip,
                                slip
to rail fate,
fail,
                         the time is late,
                              and late,
they twist,
    twist,
                          and twist,
                               spin,
        and spin,
                            sink,
          and sink;
                  hannggg.

You Are Leaving

This monstrous looming,
distant but oncoming,
like the smoke of a burning
village cloaking the landscape,
promises a razing.
                    Ash falls,
thickening in the non-light
in a courtyard deserted of footfalls.
The fountain is dry.
                    Night draws nigh.
The scent of ends chokes out "Soon, too."

Sine Qua Non—A Riddle

Riddle me this:
That without which

> the scissors feeds upon the paper made
> to hide the shattered stone of heart;

> the mightier blade no blood can draw
> lies supine in your dominion;

> the ink-black well can naught contain,
> except this howling, scrabbling pain . . .

Can you suit the sense to line and find
the three-fold death-muse clue, that

> all my pages now are blank,
> all my subjects turn to objects accusative,
> and all my poems say oblivion blue?

Unbirth

The afterbirth of our love
spills hot upon the bed.
If this is dead so soon,
then I must crawl away from you.

Wordsmouth Harbor Founder

I rage into the phone.
Heedless? No. I feel
the windlash crack the lines,
I bid the waves crash me 'gainst the pier.
The wordstorm pounds with sounds
my lips curl to form. I exult
as I hurl the handset down
into the consequences,
at last past any caring
that the relationship is sheering
its moorings and plunging
into forsaken haven danger.
(Ill the fell tongue tastes after anger
jettisons the heaviest cargo,
while the unlashed chests careen
across the lightless decks below.)
As I turn from the phone stand,
the ghost-ship heels toward the maelstrom,
rudderless, sails shredded by the gale.
As I walk down the hall, the empty hull
tips over the grimace lips and shudders
as it surrenders to the swirl.
Wracked and groaning,
cracked open past mending,
way past hailing any rescue,
I sink. I drink past drowning
the deep oblivion overhead.
I slowly settle on the bed.
I listen in the darkness to the echo
of all the reckless things I've said.

The Closedeep

So.

So I fall into the closedeep,
a zone grey of shades
and steep downslides of unfate.

The rim is way above my eyes.
The wise followed the whys
and came unruly late.

I look up yearning blue,
step back and leap,
clamber, fall, and break.

I awake and regard now the night.
I curse the far cold light
of laughing stars unsated.

I rise and try to climb again
against the wrongs you've called
too many to be enumerated.

Moving Out

With the practiced easy motion
    of hands on knobs of doors one knows,
    she hips them open and heels them closed.
        The key is on the bed.
With the sharp resolution of hands seizing bags
    she moves down the hall and out.

    In the street,
the ceaseless, jerking flow of traffic
breaks the quick insistence of her feet,
makes her lay down the bold new decisions
    at intersections
        and rest.

    In the new building,
bright patterns flicker on the tiled kitchen floor
    as gusty breezes gambol with the curtains.
Strange odors linger from some other's cooking.
The place is small but holds real promise.

The days grow longer
    with the new measure of the night.
She finds a print for the hallway wall,
    relearns the evenings for garbage,
    the taste of meals for one.
The cookbook stays open
    on the table in the sun
    and her own smells grow stronger
        with the light.

O My Heart

You and I will be very good.
We will let her get around the corner,
wait two beats, maybe three—long enough
to know for sure she's not returning.
You will lunge, then, I know.
And I will throw my arms around your neck
and grapple your howling desperation
until I've reattached the chain.
I won't let you go; no,
I will murmur something soothing,
some wordless, tuneless, hopeless—.
I will cling to your quivering
until I feel it's safe to merely rest there,
face buried to the tears
in your familiar must. The long,
long night we will sleeplessly entrust
the darkness with our pain
and wait to see: does the wrong
depart with the sunrise,
or cruelly taunt us
from the limit of your run?
But, O my heart, I promise:
I will not desert you.
I will not leave you all alone.

Love's Lost Demesne

Love's Lost Demesne

The citadel has fallen.
The touch and smell and taste of you
have breached my memory's walls.
The craven guards are all fled;
the stalwart ones are all dead
or are bleeding out. Once again,
in his tower, the keening soul laments
the sharpened sense of over—and thence
the edge of darkness calls, out there,
where emptiness breeds emptiness,
where Avalon has sunk her boats
and owls hunt the rim beyond
the knowing, name, or choice
of a lover's receding voice.
Aloneness is the spiritsap of pain,
sleeplessness the landscape
of love's lost demesne.

Snip Snap

How do these little whiskers stay
attached to the mirror, the ones
that fling out from the snip-snap
of the scissors as I trim my beard,
like the tiny hairs on gecko feet
that let them climb the walls,
some mystical surface tension thing,
or maybe static electricity,
some affinity of opposites
defying gravity—until I see them
and wipe them clear later in the day?
This is no deep mystery, not like,
what is dark energy, anyway?
No—I know why these memories of you
snip and snap at the new growth
struggling to curl up my yearning lips,
while I cling to the image I once had
of myself behind these vacant eyes
as I wipe them clear again.

I Am Holding Still

The fleet shadow shape of wings
spooks me in the twilight of a dream.
I am drifting through a silent wood
where bones of mice lie buried.
A shroud of mist, the vestige of a storm,
lifts from the chill steaming pools
around me, the water graves of memories.
Rank and dank is the gloom,
where looms the naked ribs
of a collapsing shack,
the toppled stack of a chimney.
A cracked iron pot lies canted
in the hearth amidst the ashes.
All the stones are cold,
all the timbers rotted.
Oddly, a three-legged stool
still stands beside a toppled table.
I sit my spectral self astride
and wait; for what? For what?
I am holding still
the forsaken feel of you.
When will I awaken?

Gret and Regret

I read and reread
 my young man poem
 found in a binder
 and the old flame flares
 until the decades shatter.
Through the lacerating shards
 I reach for—
  Your Facebook page
   has an old post
   about your job
   and no pictures.
  LinkedIn
   leaves me
   locked out.
But still hoping, still groping,
 I seize my pen and write.
Here I gret and regret,
 clutching close the loss.
In the middle of the night
 I wake up still bleeding.

In the Evening, Friends Come

In the evening, friends come.
When they leave, at the door
the cool, moist, leafy odor outside
surprises me with you.

Breathing, I remember

    that exciting scent I found
    around your shoulders among
    the fine nape hairs and hollows,
    the kiss of hips, and hands amove,
    every where on me alive,
    tips and palms and smooth
    dips of thigh, they rush up from the—;

    the curve of back and belly,
    the smelly curls,
    the rolling lock of legs,
    your lips, and hair flips,
    the grip and swoon of arch, and I—;

    you—

Slow subsides the surge of all
my memory's senses' songs of you,
    the touch of tooth
    upon my throat,
    the breath of air on ears,
    the—

Quiet turns the moment to the moment.
The latch falls to. It's only been a year.
I gather up the truth with the mugs,
brew a new pot of tears.

What Are We?

What Are We?

I've been alone now for how long?
Every woman I meet intrigues me.
This one's voice excites me,
this one's mind is like of mine.
Hair entangles all my arteries
and breasts sing soft songs to me.

But here in the riverworld,
the worrymind is behind me.
Right now, the water is enough.
The oak-limbs speak with breezes
over shift of green on light that ripples
in the gently curling current.

A heron laughs loose the brooding,
splashes barely as she rises.
A grey-blue feather dances down
to the calm, dimpled shimmers
in the fields of color on the water.

When the sun comes low and lies
too bright on the surface to gaze at,
the water turns to blue on black.
With its soothing voice it answers
still the call to the all-bound sea.

What are we
    but current to the pain
    and blood under tide
    of silver faces changing,
        dancing goddess moon?

I Sail, I Sail

Three times you climbed the stair
up to my loft, raised the hatch,
crept into my bed against my wishes
under cover of the night.
Woke me up to sex manipulate.
Brought me to your senses.
We were good for a time,
hot and wonton. Over all too
soon, though. But the seeds were planted.
All you really wanted, so it seems,
were the genes, the children,
a father you could count on.
So I slumbered through those years
obliviate in my assumptions.
But you hungered for more gumption,
for someone somewhere past assertion,
but short of aggression, who—.
Well. Then there he was.

I had all these ready threads
hanging from me,
waiting to be pulled.
You didn't grab them.
They just snagged on your edges
as you left.

       Bereft?
That's like saying I was
buried on the bottom of
the frigid Bering Sea,
a hint of light above
what used to be a bridge—

instead of sunken in
the utter darkness
of the Mariana Trench,
a swallow-all abyss.
Well; now that's passed.

Once the threads lay trampled
on the floor of time, and the picture
in the tapestry had faded,
and the hot brain wires
had smelted into just memories,
I picked one thread up and lo!
a pen was in my hand.
Paper had replaced the loom,
a desk made of study oak my ark.
I broke the seal on my pot of ink
and dipped into a story.
I drew pictures made of words:
a man rising somewhere
past hesitation, short of the horizon.
Not all I wrote could cast the spell
of healing. But I had hoisted
a page to the winds, opened up a hatch
and climbed aloft. I had caught a swell,
and even now I sail—I sail,
and hale the creatures on the strand
where my poems are keen to land.

Yours the New Smile

Trail Maker

Trail maker—
I want to meet you.

You swing me 'round the boles
of the bigger beeches,
then along a slope
with skinny naked trunks
and thin winter sunlight
through the open understory
slanting just so in late afternoon.

I love the little curve you made
that skirts the stone and fern here
at the bottom of the bank.

You guide me through a meadow
thick with sumac and thistle
and the smell of goldenrod,
then up into the rock formations
and passage 'round the finest angles
for surprises in the mazes.

I want to warn you, though:
that orange trail
is rank with savage rose—
one year, maybe two, before
it's strangled by the thorns.
But I suppose you know.

You take me where
the hermit thrush hen nests.

Dancing Then

I felt it, dancing then:
a sweet and vibrate body joy;
unpent chords of kenning
poured out taught between
our hips, our eyes and loins
in movements watched and learned
in rhythms found and shared
and lovely paired to fine synchronicity—
a new kind of knowing
contented to do without content,
our few words spoken coyly
soon abandoned for the growing sense
of each other's immanence,
the musical transcendence
of movement in the dance.

Yours the New Smile

Yours, the new smile, a thrill, promises
cool winds down from high places
under a bright moon changing phases,
in green-eyed pools reflected.
I heed the light-washed waters now
as too beckoning not to wade out
and see how far then could I swim
before I join the loons in their diving.

You Move Me

From the First Touch

From the first touch until now,
from the first urge and smile
into speechless roll and list,
and past the surge and crest
and smoothfit spoon resting
in spentdrift and laughter
and softtalk after, we steep,
and sleep, and even in our dreams
our gleaming body sings.

You Move Me

You move me surely,
like the sand under the hand
of tides, where the sun glows
warmly on the shift of my desire.

Etch me, then, like the grain
of wood worn in the drift
on the beach; my bare limbs
reach to embrace the lift.

Your Veryname

I almost know your veryname:
I hear some truths revealed
in the timbre of your talk.
There's a sibilant in your laughtering,
a fear in a glottal stop.
I feel a labial in the way
your hips sway when you walk.
The angle of your head just now
strokes a consonant
and speaks of curious regard.
A vowel in your hazel eyes,
long, with an accent variant,
hints at some surprise, and
all the mysteries waiting to be unsealed.

For All I'm Worth

You do dance yourself
to say your name in motion.
Yes, and dress up in its hues.
For your nomen rhythms then
I'll put on my dancing shoes
and don my no-more-blues.
I would be the space you claim
with your movements on the earth.
I would quiver, I would leap and fly,
and with my body I would cry out
who I am, too, yes, and for all I'm worth.

Writing Rite

I want to match my style to yours, to write attentive poems
with forms that honor you: direct, true, like geometry,
with lines as long, lean, and lovely as are yours,
with similes that reflect your smile. Of course
they should love to dance, these words,
with meaning choosing partners
from concrete nouns and verbs.

Each comma should have your hazel eyes to cause
the reader to pause, for drinking. For surprise
reversals, at least one dash—a hot flash
of anger unforeseen, the whole page immersed
in fire, then burning clean.

                          One stanza should contain
some little story of short-lived pain,
but then a period pronouncing that sentence served
with its tiny new moon at the end.

                          Now you deserve
a new phase; I'd write of waxing toward fullness and light,
and ask you, with my conjunction in my hand, if I may
compose alongside you, if you'll take this wedding band
of words, to start with me another strophe, one that opens

and . . .

The World Knows Its Meaning

Aloft upon Love's Wild Sea

How far ahead the road has gone!
Down from the doors of lives begun
on time's distant shores, and haply
here landed. Now opens a larger way
with promises for and from the heart,
to join two paths at the journey feet,
fuse two lives where the errands meet,
make our "whither now?" one ever art,
and stake all fortune on the mystery
of souls aloft upon love's wild sea.

The World Knows Its Meaning

Two gates open but once;
the third swings into the center.
Birth, death pass us singular,
but marriage sluices true abundance.

As two step through,
an arkful of creatures follow:
in-laws, character flaws,
secret strengths and dreams,
wisdom, patience, a whole team
of traits anticipating seasoning.

Crowding all around
are friends and relations.
Children throw flowers.
The trees clap their hands.
Stars join the celebrations.
Smiles and tears,
prayers and cheers,
rise to heaven; even
a folk poet finds a pen.

The world knows its meaning
at a wedding such as ours:
thriving, striving, diving for
the deepest precious pearl;
investing, divesting, resting in
the love-god's fingers' furl.

Union

One loop, two gyres.
One heat, two fires.

Three years now of joining
our hearts, wills, and desires.

Still fun, still good,
still rich, like food

well-prepared—this union
still thrills me and fills me
    with gratitude.

Wholly Bonded, To Be Free

How far ahead the road has gone,
down from doors of lives that started
but few degrees apart, now joined as one.
Some larger way had opened; it beckoned.
Sizable for two whose journey feet
stepped forward toward a single beacon,
to make the "whither now?" one ever art
and, face to face, heart to heart,
to stake all fortune on the mystery
of two souls wholly bonded, to be free.

You Rhyme Every Sound

Have I Missed One Day?

Has the galaxy missed one second of its revolution
in its aeons-long helical gyre?

Has the heliacal blaze of the sun missed one explosion
in its chemistry of starfire?

Do the sea's cool currents offshore miss the swarms
of albacore, or the whales the silence of the sails?

Do the skies miss the hours-long passage of flocks
of passenger pigeon plumage against the blue?

Have I missed our bodies' hymnal praise under moon,
or one single day bearing this longing?

Only every moment since you've been away.

You Rhyme Every Sound

I see no other eyes than yours.
Your skin my hands do woo.
I ascend into your savory scent
and taste the tang of lavender.
All my senses ever sated,
you release each time into now.
You rhyme every sound with your vow,
and I, with my lips and tongue,
oh I do, too.

Turning Fifty

Like the shadows in a Caravaggio
your age names your beauty.
A seasoned grace has claimed your face
and deepened your eyes at fifty.

Answers with a Grin

A quiet melancholy sometimes falls upon me,
all unbidden by any pesky circumstance.
I do not shake it off, I do not try.
I lie in wait instead, watchful in the dim.
Some new air will stir the leaves around me,
spread them open for a view of you
staring off—some ingenious recipe
for honey mustard dressing homing in.
Or who knows what blessing bends your brow
and curls your lips up ever so slightly?
But here it is: a beam falling through the canopy
onto a pool a-ripple with some hidden presence
in the depths, a figure of our love a-move,
rising to the surface of my heart;
and above, however haggard or laggard
my other selves might be,
this one lifts his face up to the bright
and answers with a grin at the sight.

Gratitudesong

I sing a song of gratitude
for you, Christine Marie;
for the tiller of my soul,
I raise this homely jubilee—

for your mindful love of bodies,
our holiness and beauty,
our wholeness and purity,
our life-depending intimacy
with sun and seed and soil;

how frying pans and fires,
broccoli rabe and the gyres
of the seasons all haphazardly
conspire to produce for us
the most ambrosial board on earth,
for you, the mistress
of serendipitous taste;

and how expressive you are,
like a riot bed of tulips;
like a blast of nasturtium
upon the tongue, you splash
immoderate upon the world,
full of humor and surprise;

a London plane tree, you are,
honest as a snowstorm in April,
faithful as a thaw,
as giving as compost,
hard-working as the winds,
forward-planning as a seed list,
vigilant for slugs, for all life's
moral adversaries—deep
with character are you;

and what a character you are:
you dance with poles and beans,
with flowers and floors,
with life's more uncommon
rhythms and tunes, you dance,
with verve, with friends
you move with loyal grace,
and with me—
you dance with me.

As a man who, hungry,
eats his fill at last,
I render my tender thanks.
For into your gardens
late in my summer
I stepped. We danced.
Then out of the coming frost
you plucked me;
fresh to your table you fed me
arugula—arugula;
I'd never even heard the word
back then.
Somehow, though,
I knew how new
all life would soon become.
I took my place at table.
Now—as then—and since,
I say my grace:

Thank you, God,
for the "I do" that filled my pod,
for Christine, Christine Marie.

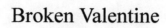

Broken Valentine

I'm Sorry I Gave You Such a Fright

I'm sorry I gave you such a fright
when I stayed out late last night
and didn't call. I was out carousing,
that's all—dancing, drinking,
having a ball. What a surprise
to find the cops in the kitchen
asking whether I drop in at bars
very often.

Broken Valentine, Whole-hearted

Awfully hard on hearts
these months and years
of toil and tears, and too many
enemies and too few reprieves,
of grievous last goodbyes without relent.

But the firmament still turns,
spinning stars through the night.
The snow lies bright over hidden seeds.
And I—I stumble along beside you,
sharing a portion of the pain
and caring about the sum;
trying to be steadfast,
a sharpness of starlight
crossing the vastest dark
to reach you, however dim
and blinking at the last.

Metaphors, I know,
not the concrete actions
that would show, and not just beg.
So—a broken valentine, yes.
But a whole heart inside,
striving to guide with best intent
my hands and brains
in marriage sacrament.

Marmots

Interrupting a perfectly pleasant
hypnagogic reverie,
you spoke, and woke me:
Steven, why don't you go to bed?
Why? said I.
Because it looks like your neck will break
and let go of your head, or something.
I closed my eyes again.
I had been daydreaming
of pulling the ears off rabbits.
It was Easter; nearly.
But marriage is all about compromise,
and you meant well.
I thought about switching to badgers,
but I'm not sure what badgers look like, really.
I just know they have something to do
with mad cow disease.
So I went to work on marmots.

Not Quite Ready Yet

I vigorously pump the milk foamer,
alone with my coffee in the study,
the closest I'll get to sex
for who knows how long.
You sleep. Up for hours in the night,
alone with your list of grievances,
you soon will rise bleary-eyed,
not quite ready yet
to fight again that wrong.

The Rise and Surprise of You

I'm amazed at what
a good night's sleep can do.
The shadows have mostly fled
into the corners of the day.
They're not gone, of course.
You might just awake
and seek them out. Or maybe not.
We shall see. As for me,
I pass my yearning pen
across the open page
to write my heart anew.
And that's not all I've got.
I have the fire at the source,
the ring upon my finger, and
the knowing of how to find my way.
So I write and I patiently await
the rise and daily surprise of you.

Clearer Skies

The storm passes, the sun rises.
The anger we find has faded.
It lingers, yes, not forgotten,
nor ignored; but it belongs
to yesterday, to all the ready
yesterdays that still clutch
their memories of our wrongs
in the vault of all our faults.
We keep the key on the dresser
in the shadow that our love-lamp casts
from our joyous wedding picture.
We leave it there untouched today,
letting "I'm sorry" heal, somewhat,
some of our sorrow, and looking forward
to clearer skies this morrow.

Change Is a Grace

To some vexatious degree,
you are who you are,
and I am I, and we are we.
Change often is a grace
come all unexpectedly
upon some mystery
of divine intervention—
I at least cannot divine it.
Acceptance is the key,
they say. In the meantime,
we struggle on through each other's
faults and noisome bothers,
face to face with a mild
and intermittent misery—
and not so mild, sometimes.
But we know that, in a while,
our smiles will break through,
and over this long ensue
the green will outlast
the black and the blue.

Weather Another Storm

The tree's branches bend to meet the light.
Each one follows its own jagged path,
and not all survive the winds or weight of snow.
But the roots go deep to stand against the bedrock,
to slip into the cracks and grip to stabilize the whole.
My soul follows, seeking out the hollows there,
where parts of me are missing.
They make you angry; they give me sorrow;
they send us harrowing into hell, sometimes.
But you are not without your faults and fissures,
either. Neither of us forgets, however,
the bedrock and the light, and all the rings
that count our years together, bearing such fruit,
sending out new shoots after howling winter's
bare branches have weathered another storm.

The Very Best Part

Here We Are

It's not easy being married to
a fierce women's liberationist,
a warrior harried for a lifetime,
hard tempered by losing battles.
For, as a man, I share some faults
and traits with all those men
who throw up and then defend
the barriers your fists descend upon
with such relentless fury.
Sometimes the wall you pound
stands inside my own mind,
and in your rage I find I hear
the sound of my own name.

Between our learning hearts, however,
a single moral compass swings.
And through it all, here we are,
still walking hand in hand,
bound on this winding journey by
these weathered wedding bands.
May I always hunger for your fire
and heave my threshed and winnowed tares
upon our covenanted pyre.

The Siren of the Flesh

The siren of the flesh
no longer hits the high Cs,
but she is far from silent.

Her tongue has ears for the harmonies,
for the desire in the fire of you in me,
for the phrasing and timing and yearning
over years of learning each other's song.

It rises up full and rich
in a husky seasoned alto;
it needs no higher pitch

to call to the deeper draw of current
or the crashing swells, to unleash
the body lashed to the mast. I stumble
to the rudder and heel the vessel over.

It shudders. I laugh. I lean
into the yaw and aim
the plunging prow for shore.

The Very Best Part

Anniversary
twenty-one—
not on the surface
a very auspicious year.
One could slumber,
or lumber right past
its quiet place of power
as the count of days
in an old gibbous moon—
no longer full, not yet new,
halfway between replete and
the birth of our next phase,
its promises hidden in its shadow bower.
Meanwhile: lots of lopsided light,
bright enough to see our way
through the nights and days before us,
walking side by side, remembering
how good it is we wed.
But enough, already—
all this moony stuff
is just inside my head.
The real organ of the hour
is my heart:
my abiding love for you
is, of these my later days,
the very best part.

Heaven to Steven

Three things feed the roots of my heart,
   four things speed me to bloom:

all forms of stone, the cliffs and caves
   and mysteries of the All-Mother's bones;

also fire, the tare consumer and transform fuse
   as muse, spirit enchanter of tongues;

Beethoven's Ninth and all Tchaikovsky,
   Dylan and Hendrix and Clapton;

any true worth, shaped with art
   to marry the Maker to the made;

the mockingbird, who dances as he sings,
   and all the soaring people with their wings;

good work, hard work, callouses on the hands,
   the ridge beam placed just so;

and you my love, my wife and life, the seventh,
   the fullest blessing of heaven to Steven.

What Is Heaven?

And what is heaven, to Steven?
Not some transcendental region
that beckons from some distant when,
but a reach into the lives we live
right here and now of a light that dwells
within us and between us,
that illuminates the why and the how
of being more fully human,
more present to each other.
This light penetrates even
the most persistent overcast.
Being more whole is its goal;
not perfection, but some good direction,
that knows the world as it really is,
and as it could be, as it should be.
This heaven holds my lover's heart
in hands intent on healing,
on holding one another steadfast
against the winds of the storms inevitable.
This heaven caresses with its light,
it blesses without condition. It listens,
and it answers our human cries
with strength and truth and wisdom
in measure just enough to keep us
on the path, and then some,
for all the trials, yes, and all the joys
that we know are still to come.
In this covenant of convergence
and emergence, in this spiral open ring,
it is love that raises with its uplift
toward the better, and marriage
that turns always to the center,

returning over and ever to each other,
in spite of—because of—all the obstacles,
faults, failures, and diversions,
in one long occasion for thanksgiving.

About the Author

Steven Dale Davison has published poems in more than two dozen journals. Mr. Davison has published three other books of poetry: a full-length collection of "nature" poems titled *Dancing Mockingbird* (Kelsay Books); a hybrid book of poetry and images, *The Road to Continental Heart: Befriending, and Defending, the Spirit of North America* (Boyle and Dalton); and *O My Heart,* a chapbook (Moonstone Press). Several of his plays have been produced, including several written in verse. He has written both short and long fiction and has published a number of nonfiction essays and book chapters. An active Quaker, Mr. Davison has a nonfiction Quaker book under contract with Inner Lights Books. Mr. Davison worked for twenty years as a journalist and professional writer in the private sector and now writes for himself full-time. He lives in Pennington, New Jersey, with his wife Christine M. Lewandoski.